DIVORCE 911

TOP LAWYERS REVEAL THEIR #1 TIPS FOR COUPLES CALLING IT QUITS

AF808047

Andy R. Curry

Seven Falls Publishing

ISBN-13: 978-0692746325
ISBN-10: 0692746323

The publisher of this book is generously donating all royalties from the retail sales of "**DIVORCE 911**" to:

Interfaith Hospitality Network

The mission of Family Promise of Colorado Springs is to end family homelessness in our community one family at a time.

Family Promise realizes its mission by providing transitional shelter and supportive services to homeless families and those at immediate risk to experience homelessness. Family Promise's primary goal is to assist families with children to permanently transition into independent affordable housing; secondary goals include meeting community transitional housing needs in the most cost-effective manner possible and providing congregations with an opportunity to put their faith into action.

Family Promise's core program is The Interfaith Hospitality Network, which derives its name from our numerous partnerships with area congregations that provide shelter and direct support to homeless families; the network includes congregations of diverse faiths and denominations. However, Family Promise provides services to all families with children regardless of person

You can learn more about IHN by visiting

http://www.ihn-cos.org/

This book was made possible by tips from the following:

Andrew Vaughn, Attorney at Law

Annette Fernholz, Attorney at Law

Belinda C. Brown, Attorney at Law

Bernard Rinella, Attorney at Law (Firm of Rinella and Rinella)

Bob Downs, Partner with Downs McCarthy Law Group

Elain Smith, Partner at Smith & Horwitz, A Philadelphia Family Law Firm Limited To Domestic Relations

Evie Jeang, Attorney at Law

Fran Brochstein, Attorney and Mediator

Irene Intelligator, Attorney at Law

James Robertson, Attorney at Law

John Bo Nichols, Attorney at Law

John R. Benson Attorney at Law

Judy Ritts, Texas Attorney at Law

Kurt Muller, Attorney at Law

Maria Testa, Attorney at Law

Mark A. Reed, Esq

Michael Griffin, Attorney at Law

Miles Beermann, Beerman Law

Paul F. Moore II, Attorney at Law

Paul J. Duron, Attorney at Law

Rebecca Cornia, Attorney at Law

Rick Marsh, Attorney at Law

Scott D. Reiner, Attorney at Law

Seth D. Kramer, Esq CFLS (Certified Family Law Specialist)

Sheryl Johnson-Todd, Attorney at Law

Stephen Lekas, Attorney

Thomas Ferreira, Attorney Mediator

CONTENTS

FOREWORD

It's unfortunate that divorce is not spelled with four letters to make it a four-letter word because divorce is ugly no matter where either party is at in the process. If there are children, they suffer even if the divorce is amicable (which is somewhat of a conflict in terms). Even if children are not part of the equation, the ugliness will still likely rear its head. If it doesn't, consider yourself fortunate because that is out of the norm.

This book is meant to help anyone just starting divorce up through someone being in the middle of it. You will learn divorce tips from actual attorneys who specialize in divorce. You will get ideas of what to do and what not to do.

The information garnered in this book was obtained by interviewing divorce attorneys. Their responses were transcribed and lightly edited as we wanted you to see their responses as if you were talking to them face to face.

CHAPTER ONE

THE BIG TAKE AWAY – WHAT EVERY READER MUST KNOW

As a divorcee myself, I have experience in the dark world of a relationship gone bad. The emotions that fly in the face of reason are often out of the ordinary. I remember having so much contempt that I couldn't care less what happened to my soon-to-be-ex spouse. I didn't care if she was broke. I didn't care if she was homeless. I didn't care if she was sick. I just didn't care – period.

Before you judge me, you should know I'm nothing like that. I care a great deal for people. As far as my ex-spouse today, I do hope she's happy and healthy. Yet at the time of being in the midst of the ugliness, I didn't care.

When you don't care, the reasons are the justification for the rage one feels. She did this, he did that. Then you, as the soon-to-be divorcee, will talk to anyone who will listen. You feel so violated by the other person that you tell any bent ear the woes and end your conversation with "Can you believe that?!!!"

I remember seeing an old friend from my High School class one day sitting in his car at a drive in restaurant in town. I just pulled up to order and there he was right across from me. It had been several years since I saw him but he certainly looked much the same. I waved. He waved. I ordered my food. Then I slipped out of my car to go say hi.

"What have you been up to?" I asked. He said, "Well, I just moved back to town about a week ago after my divorce was finalized so I'm getting back on my feet again."

Now to me, that was, in a strange way, music to my ears because I was near the end of my divorce. I was still reeling in mental anguish. He was still feeling the pain from his divorce and I was still fresh in mine. That's when I discovered how two people who hardly know each other are brought together as friends by a common enemy – divorce.

We swapped war stories and consoled each other for the egregious misdeeds done against us. Never mind that he or I might have been complete asses ourselves in our marriages. That didn't matter. What mattered is we had someone listening who had been there and understood the injustice of it all and would side with us by saying things like, "Wow! That's terrible. I can't believe she did that to you!" Ahhh. To hear someone agree with us who has been there and had the same kind of thing done to them is sweet, sweet music.

To this day, he and I are still friends. We talk about once a week but we almost never discuss the divorce issues because it's old and negative. Who wants to keep reliving that?

However, when I was going through the divorce there were roadblocks and obstacles thrown in my face that I never dreamed would've happened. In other words, I had no foresight of what was to come.

For instance, although I was feeling powerful and cocky by not having to be part of her life anymore, I was also unsure, not confident about meeting other women, drinking excessively, gaining weight, and generally unhappy in lots of ways.

I remember being so glad to be rid of her negativity that I thought, "I am ONE ELIGIBLE BACHELOR! I'll have women wanting to go out with me right and left." I was the manager of a well-known business in a small town. I knew most folks and they knew me. Yet, my door was not beat down by anxious girls as I had imagined. You may think I'm crazy to admit that but the fact is, it's one of the thoughts I dreamed up in the midst of divorce. I point it out because in divorce all kinds of things happen. Your situation will be unique to you. Except for nefarious actions, it's perfectly normal and acceptable to feel all that negativity. The trick is, knowing what's normal and getting out of the negativity and getting on with life.

Barring that, I want you to hear from lots of different divorce lawyers because each has their own experience on dealing with many, many couples calling it quits. You'll notice the interesting differences in their tips. Also, they are from different states in the U.S. and their laws will differ from state to state yet, you'll read very sound recommendations on how to handle yourself.

I wish I would've had this guide when I was getting divorced because there is a ton of great information here. I will admit that some of the words of wisdom would've been hard to swallow because while I was so angry and bitter at times, I would've had a hard time being cordial as you see are one of the recommendations. It turns out that being cordial is a great divorce tool but it is DAMN hard to do when you feel rage.

The last thing I want to say is an eye-popper revealed to me by a divorce lawyer. He and I were discussing his life as a lawyer. I offhandedly asked how he dealt with the constant negativity of divorcing couples. He said this to me: *You know, I've often thought of going back to being a criminal attorney because your client is often a bad person on their best behavior. A divorce client is typically a good person on their worst behavior.*

CHAPTER TWO

WHAT IF SOMEONE IS GETTING DIVORCED?

Tip from Andrew Vaughn, Attorney at Law

The first thing I would do is ask them two questions. The first question is, "Were you married?" We ask that question because there are two different categories of family law for couples who are married, or couples who had children together but weren't married. Then, once we find out they were married, we find out if they had children or didn't have children. If they had children, then there are five potential issues that we need to address in their case in Illinois. If they didn't have children, then there are two potential issues that we have to address.

Alternatively, if they were not married but did have children, then we have at least three to four issues that we would have to address for them. Again, start from that base line of "how many issues are we really dealing with here?" Then, once we go through that process, one of the things that we advise our clients is to get as educated as humanly possible. In addition to my background of being an attorney and having an MBA and doing some of the more advanced financial side of the divorce litigation, a lot of people refer to me as a divorce attorney for multi-millionaires, where I do high-level financial divorce. For many of my clients, they still need an education on what divorce means. We actually rope in my background as a law school professor to help with that.

In terms of the most important advice that we give right at the very beginning, it's to get as educated as you can about this, and we'll help you with that. We then walk our clients through the issues that they have in their case, what the law is on that, any anticipated changes in that law, which is something we're going through right now in Illinois where there's a new divorce statute coming down the pipe.

"Get as educated as you can about this"

Then talking through where they can find additional resources, we have an e-book, we have a divorce dictionary, we have a number of things that we provide our clients, or other great places to get those educational resources if it's not through us.

Tip from Bob Downs, Partner with Downs McCarthy Law Group

The number one thing is, don't be afraid to ask questions. You should go in with a list of ten questions. Any ten questions you want, for example, do you represent more men than women? How much do you charge? How you do your billing? How long have you been practicing? How many cases have you tried? Those are just some representative questions.

I wrote up a sheet for this for an organization in Cook County called the Lilac Group that does lawyer referral. The real thing is, it doesn't matter so much what the answers are, but it gives the client the edge of getting to know the lawyer by how they answer those questions. It is almost a marital relationship that can go sour just like marriages. Too many people are either too trusting or they're afraid to ask questions. That's not a good way to start.

It also isolates the client somewhat from the lawyer's pitch. He's used to welcoming mister and missus into his office to sit down. Then, he goes right into his or her routine. This breaks that up. The lawyer should sell himself at something more than generalities. We're very experienced. I know all the judges. Don't worry about anything, we'll take care of it. That's just telling the client what they want to hear. Many clients, that's what they want to hear. They don't really learn anything about the lawyer.

My number one piece of advice, is don't be afraid to ask questions. You're more likely to find out whether it's a good fit or not. If you charge in increments of a tenth of an hour or a quarter of an hour? How much do you charge for a typical telephone call? It's okay to talk about money. Everybody's afraid to talk about money.

Do you have paralegals and law clerks that do routine things? Do you itemize in your billing? Every lawyer should do those things.

"Too many people are either too trusting or they're afraid to

ask questions. That's not a good way to start."

You can't collect on a fee petition in Illinois without in fact itemizing the day you did it, exactly what you did. In other words, an entry telephone call with client .3 or whatever it might be, will be thrown out in a fee petition. You have to say what the phone call was about. Then, put down how much time. That's itemized billing.

Even now, a lot of lawyers still don't do itemized billing. Particularly in family law it's very important because fee disputes are often very frequent. Something I feel strongly about in regard to clients is learning more about the lawyer. If they haven't got a resume or website then be careful. What have they done?

I believe strongly in specialties. In some states, Illinois included, you cannot claim family law as any kind of a specialty. Other states you can. Then they have certification requirements for it. We don't have that in Illinois. You want a lawyer that does this regularly for three reasons: You want them to know the law, you want them to know the procedure and every bit as important is, know the practical facts of life of that jurisdiction.

As I said, talking about men and women representation.

There's more variance of how judges run their calls than any other variable factor. An experienced lawyer who is in those parts all the time, knows ten times more than the lawyer who thinks he can handle a divorce. It's no place for a general practitioner.

Tip from Miles Beermann, Beerman Law

In most cases there are children, and I stress no matter who's sitting in front of me, the father or the mother, that you got to strive to have a good divorce, because you're tied up with your spouse for the rest of your life. A lot of people don't get that. They want to get away from the person, and they don't realize that they have children together, and they've got to be together at family functions, some good and some bad. We stress that here.

As far as the process goes, most lawyers that I know will start the process with a letter to the opposing party telling them that we hope to settle the case and asking that they please have their lawyer contact us. We don't usually serve papers on anybody. Hopefully we all know each other in Chicago, even though it's a big town, and what we found out is who their lawyer is and we sent the papers to the lawyer, and the lawyer files an appearance and we're off and running. The process involves complete disclosure of all assets and all income, so that both parties have the same information. We guard against anybody who we're representing withholding any information, and we do our best to get information from the other side that gives us a total and complete picture of what's happening.

That's the beginning of the case. Then, if there aren't any kids, it gets in the way. You know, you go back to the old days; and I'm going way back. I'm probably the oldest practicing divorce lawyer in Chicago who's still active.

I've been doing this for fifty-seven years, and what you found in the old days was if a man came to see you, maybe the man told his wife, "You're not going to get a penny." The woman tells her husband, "You're never going to see your kids again." You know, it's all bullshit. Obviously, it doesn't happen.

"You've got to strive to have a good divorce, because you're tied up with your

spouse for the rest of your life."

You've been there, you know that doesn't happen, or it shouldn't happen, and so if somebody has that attitude, do your best to disabuse them. Also, you have to be very careful about telling people what really is going to happen, as opposed to what you think they want to hear. Because if you start telling people what you think they want to hear, you're going to get yourself in a bad situation with a client, because you can't deliver at that point.

Tip from Stephen Lekas, Attorney

That depends a lot on whether it's a child custody situation or not. It also depends if it's just a property situation or both. That's basically how I classify them. I classify them as children, non-children. That makes a big difference.

For the sake of argument, let's classify it as children and property.

"Possession is nine-tenths of the law, and usually, whoever has possession at the time it goes to

court usually ends up getting custody unless their possession is through illegal means."

If it's a custody, then, hopefully, they have the children in their custody versus if they don't have the children in their custody. I would need to know why because the courts tend to look at, by the time you get to court, who has the children in their custody and how long and why. There is, I guess, the old saying that possession is nine-tenths of the law, and usually, whoever has possession at the time it goes to court usually ends up getting custody unless their possession is through illegal means or whatever.

As for property, obviously, if it's real estate, you don't really have a whole lot to worry about. If it's bank accounts, you definitely need to make sure they are secure. If you don't get a restraining order, you need to open up your own account or get out of being a joint account because, typically, one side or the other ends up draining those accounts. At least, that's what I've seen. It's hard to get that back later.

Tip from John R. Benson Attorney at Law

The first thing is that it's not about winning. With family law nobody wins their case. It's all about cutting your losses.

The second thing is that the judge doesn't care about you. What I mean by that is that the judge isn't trying to figure out how good of a person you are or how bad you think the other person is. The judge doesn't really care about you or the other side. All the judge really cares about is the children. That's the focus of everything: from the child's point of view.

"With family law nobody wins their case. It's all about

cutting your losses."

I usually say that when people are telling me about all the bad things that the other person has done, such as, "Oh, he slept with prostitutes. He cheated on me. He did this. He did that," or, "She's been doing all these horrible things. I can't believe what she's doing to me. She's trying to take my child away from me." These are the typical things that I hear every day. When I tell people that it's not about winning, people do relax, and they often tell me that they were going to try to hit the other side, try to hurt the other side, try to get him or get the house. "I'm going to make it tough on them."

Then, when I tell them it's not about winning, it seems to, if they are listening and can process that, make it much easier for them, and we can get to what really happens in family court which is just talking property, setting the visitation schedules, and changing their status from married to single. It's really that simple and that uncomplicated. When people's emotions get involved, it does get very complicated, and it always does. It's a very emotional, irrational process.

Tip from James Robertson, Attorney at Law

Leaving the kids out of it is the main thing, and don't do anything you don't want the judge to hear.

Most people mess up by Facebook and other social media, and that's part of what I'm saying when I say don't put anything out there that you won't want the judge to hear.

"Don't do anything you don't want the judge to hear."

In a case I once worked, there was a Facebook post with a child in a picture with them having a drink in their hand. They had been complaining about the other side's alcohol abuse. I see people having Facebook pictures of them supposedly smoking marijuana, texting the other side and being verbally abusive, just cursing at them through text and emails, when they talk about the other side. These are both child custody issues and property issues too.

Tip from Kurt Muller, Attorney at Law

The first thing that we try to do is determine whether or not somebody really wants a divorce. Now, I know that sounds kind of silly because you think by the time somebody invests thirty dollars to park their car, five hundred dollars to see a lawyer for a consultation, at least it is in our case, that they pretty much have a mindset as to what they want to do. But that's not necessarily true.

A lot of times, people don't know what they want. They need some direction. I'd say out of every hundred people that come in through our door, there's probably five or six that aren't really sure they want a divorce. They haven't really thought it through correctly. They know that they're unhappy but they don't know that they are dealing with it in the proper way.

We try to therapy it out because I don't like to encourage anybody to get a divorce unless they absolutely, positively know that that's what they want. So, part of the interview process is to determine how long somebody's been married, the children that they have, the assets that they have, the debts that they have, and then what other issues are facing their marriage. Then, after about a half an hour or so of an interview, it generally leads to the question, "Are you sure you really want this divorce?"

Or, sometimes I conclude that I can't conclude from what people are saying, that maybe they don't. I'm not saying that that's the case in most cases, but once in a while, we want to find out if there's a possibility that somebody can salvage their marriage, can try to reconcile with their spouse, or maybe try to just understand what the problem is.

People have problems they can't articulate, then they can't communicate them properly and this is an issue of communication or an issue of misunderstanding or maybe it's just a pure issue of control. People feel they're out of control. They have no control; they have no say. If it's a question of identifying those issues, then we may direct somebody to do things other than get a divorce, like go to more marriage counselors or proceed to some mediation. So, that's one of the first steps that we take.

For the people that still want to get a divorce, if they can be very clear that that's what they want, I always ask them, "Do you still love your husband? Do you still love your wife?" Somebody says that they still love their wife or they still love their husband, I have always believed that they should be able to find some reasons to make their marriage work rather than to get a divorce.

But if somebody's concluded that they don't love their spouse anymore and that they absolutely can't stand that person and they absolutely want to get a divorce, then it goes to the next level. Now, the next level is, is it going to be a divorce that can be settled easily? Is it something that somebody should mediate? Is it something that somebody should collaborate with other lawyers on to try and reach a simple settlement that will save them the time and the stress of going to court and having to litigate things on an ongoing basis? Or are they married to somebody that's completely unreasonable that just needs to be taught a lesson by taking them to court a bunch of times?

Because the bottom line is, if people know that they don't love their spouse, people haven't reconciled and have gotten to the point where they know they want a divorce, then they have to make a decision whether they can settle it. If they can't settle it, then they're going to have to fight it. Most divorces ultimately settle. I'm sure you know that from your work speaking to other attorneys. Ninety-eight percent of cases that are filed wind up being settled before they are concluded in a trial.

"Divorce is always about control. Somebody has control. Somebody doesn't have control. Somebody wants control. Somebody tries to take control away. Somebody's trying

to control the other person. That's always what a divorce ultimately is about."

Of the two percent that go to trial, they are particularly vitriolic kinds of cases. Sometimes they involve custody. Sometimes they involve money. They always involve ego. They always involve ego and a need for control. Ultimately, divorces are not about money. They're not about children. They're not about sex or in-laws or the color that the wall should be painted. They're always about control. Somebody has control. Somebody doesn't have control. Somebody wants control. Somebody tries to take control away. Somebody's trying to control the other person. That's always what a divorce ultimately is about.

That is going to lead either to a settlement or it's going to lead into a battle to the bitter end. So, the interview process is really the important point in somebody's initiation of proceedings because it defines who they are and what they are ultimately looking for and how they can accomplish it in the best way. Or if they can't, then how they need to gear up for a battle that may go several months, some years, and cost tens of thousands of dollars.

Tip from Thomas Ferreira, Attorney Mediator

The number one, overarching tip is settle the case. Don't sweat the small stuff. Just settle. Try not to engage in the battle because, frequently, it's more expensive and more upsetting than it's worth. Usually, the thing you're fighting over is not as valuable as what you're going to spend trying to get it.

"Settle the case. Usually, the thing you're fighting over is not as valuable as what

you're going to spend trying to get it."

I would say tip number two would be to plan ahead and know what you want going in. That's especially true in child custody cases. I see over and over again in family court people saying to the judge, "Okay, you decide." That's just not going to work. Generally, when you have child custody cases, it's important to know exactly what parenting plan that you think is good for the children and be able to articulate child-focused reasons why that's a good parenting plan. That's far better than just throwing it up to the court.

The same thing goes for the financial aspects of the case. I advise people to get a spreadsheet, get their documents together, and understand exactly what it is that they are going for and what outcome they want. See the end from the beginning so to speak. Then, when questions come up, they're Johnny on the spot with answers. You're acting instead of reacting.

Another tip is to let go of the need for revenge. Let go of the need to somehow vindicate yourself. This system is, by design, unjust in the sense that it doesn't really matter whose fault anything is. It's supposed to run like a formula. Usually, people that are involved in divorce litigation are holding on to some aspect of the relationship through the litigation. You’ve got to let it go. Make a clean break. Establish a very strong boundary between the two worlds. I like to quote that George Herbert saying, "The best revenge is living well."

Tip from Elain Smith, Partner at Smith & Horwitz, A Philadelphia Family Law Firm Limited To Domestic Relations

Assuming the couple is not yet separated, clearly there has to be a plan in terms of how you approach the other spouse and what you're going to say. They need to plan the actual conversation about the breakup, that's one thing. Second of all, they need to get as many financial records and stuff together as possible because there are going to be issues, so they're going to need tax returns and copies of deeds and leases and things of that sort. It's good to have financial documents handy so they're not going helter-skelter looking around.

"There has to be a plan in terms of how you approach the other spouse

and what you're going to say."

If there are children, obviously the person has to have some ideas about what they think an ideal arrangement would be. If they're going to live nearby, it's certainly best for children if the parents live near each other. There's a lot of things.

Therapy is very helpful, I think, for people going through a divorce. There's a wide range of experiences. Some people have been living separate and apart under one roof for years and some people it's a total surprise that their spouse wants out. You really need to see where the parties are, see where your client is, then you can give them some kind of realistic advice, in terms of making that first step.

Tip from Sheryl Johnson-Todd, Attorney at Law

My number one tip would be to take a survey about what your assets and liabilities are while you still have access to whatever computer the spouse uses, and to search it for assets and liabilities, and of course, you might pick up other things at the same time, but the primary goal would be to pick up assets and liabilities before one of them walks out of the house with the computer and the pass code. I think that's probably the most significant thing.

"Take a survey about what your assets and liabilities are while you still have access to whatever computer the spouse uses."

I also urge people to do a really big sweep with their accountant, if they have one, to understand what liabilities may be out there. They need to get a firm idea of where they stand. So many people come to the lawyer and say, "Oh, well, I don't know anything about that," and by that time, the other spouse has shut down the computer, changed the codes, and whatever, and then you have a much more difficult time trying to put it all together again. You might not ever be able to do that. Ever.

I think that's the number one tip. I also really ask people to search their conscience about whether or not any type of counseling, either professional or religious or otherwise, might help them see why the marriage is falling apart, and what might be done on their behalf. They can only change themselves, but some people just haven't thought outside of the box. They're so angry at whatever behavior they've encountered. I believe that checking the finances to know where you really are is critical because so many people do not know where they are. It seems that it's even more so for wives who don't manage finances.

I guess with regard to finances, that's kind of the primary one. Of course, your negative side of things, you can tell people about how they can do some "divorce planning". What I mean by that is that if you really want a Jaguar or an airplane or a boat, go buy it, because once you drive it off the dealership parking lot or float it out of the harbor, it loses value instantaneously, no matter if you drive it a mile. Basically, the other spouse is going to be paying for a portion of that.

Basically, what happens in Texas in a contentious divorce, it can last 18 months to two years. I just finished one up this morning that has been on the books for 26 months now. During the course of 26 months, the community would have been paying off whatever this luxury item is. In the end, the chances that the other spouse wants your boat or fishing boat or your airplane or your car is slim. You end up getting it, and you get it at blue book value, so that the community's taken a hit for the expensive nature of the item.

The other thing, in this day and time, is I tell my clients to shut down all their social media, period. The end. No question.

Quit it. Stop it. Go without it during the course of the divorce. People in their mid-30s, they can't get off of the machines, and so they end up really kicking themselves in the fanny with the pictures and the tweets and the Facebooks, and all that, it will come back to haunt them. Now that we've really been heavy into this for two or three years, it still fascinates me. If you read through 300 people's Facebooks posts, what they say is like being a boy with hormones raging, and you're a junior in high school. It's like they just have to jump in and say the most smart alec, stupid thing, but it will come back to hurt them. I tell them to stop all social media, period.

Tip from John Bo Nichols, Attorney at Law

First, they come to me and they haven't separated and are wondering if they should get a divorce, as a fundamental policy of mine I never answer that question because that's their call. I won't be the one to sit there and say, "Get a divorce." Once they decide to go that route, then I'm the means to the end. Once they've decided to go that route, and they've concluded I'm getting a divorce but I haven't moved out of the house, what I typically tell them is this. If they're leaving the house, they need to start evidencing property which means making a list or an inventory of what's there. I typically have them do a video walkthrough of the house, opening all the closets and doors, videoing things, and so on. And I have them start downloading information that's on the family computers and software and accounts which they have been given the passwords for before they file the divorce, that way there is an accountability to where if we file divorce and the other spouse starts changing passwords and locks them out of the house or taking property out of the house and putting it in storage, or putting it with someone else, we can track it and recreate the estate. That's important for taking inventory.

The other thing I have them do prior to their separation is if they've decided to get a divorce, to sit down with their spouse. After they've got the information and inventory, sit down with their spouse and try to make that spouse realize that they need to let their children know that even though mommy and daddy can't be together, it doesn't mean they still can't be a great mommy and daddy. A level of love and respect drew us together in the beginning of our relationship, let's try and tap into that and understand that that was there at the end of our relationship. The reason why I have them have that conversation is because the more they can control the destiny of the case, three things are going to happen: Number one, there's no easier decision to live with than your own decision. Number two, it's going to save you a lot of money and if kids are involved, and most importantly, it sets a good precedent for the parties being able to communicate and co-parent for the sake of the children once they're no longer in the same household.

So one is an inventory. Once they've done the inventory, sit down and have the conversation with the other spouse, and the other is I have them start putting together documents for me that I need like a chronology to bring me up to speed as to how we got to this point in your marriage where you want a divorce. What are the facts that have happened? Basically a detailed summary so that I can learn as their story teller and as their salesperson, I can learn what's in the book before I go try to pitch it. In addition, I tell them to figure out a way to focus on their health, the health of their children, and their work and retire the problem to me. And the reason why I have them do that first, so that they already have enough stress and anxiety, they need to retire it to their attorney to an extent so they can focus on their health and wellbeing. But there's another reason why the attorneys typically have the clients do that from the beginning and that is we don't have a personal stake in it. Because we don't have a personal stake in it, we're able to remove ourselves objectively and remain objectively grounded and that's what you want your attorney to do.

Part of it is information gathering, part of it is starting negotiations with the other side, or setting the ground work of trying to make it as amicable as possible. Part of it is mental and emotional, just making them realize that there's a reason why they're paying the attorney the money that they are to take care of this and they need to release it to us.

Tip from Rebecca Cornia, Attorney at Law

My top advice would be that they sit down with an attorney and do a financial analysis of how divorce could affect them. A lot of people don't realize that the rules on who pays spousal support, how long it's paid for and how assets are divided, can vary from case to case and a good attorney can help a client to prepare before the divorce is filed so that client is in the strongest possible position.

"Do a financial analysis of how divorce could affect you."

Tip from Mark A. Reed, Esq

First, I try to tell them to put their emotions aside or, at least, keep them in check, which will, eventually, save a lot of anguish and grief in the long run. When people are married, especially for a long time, they let their emotions get involved, and they want to either hurt the other person, punish them, or argue over stupid things, which mean nothing, and it ends up costing them more money than it's really worth. It causes more aggravation.

"Try not to be so emotional."

That's what I pretty much try to tell everyone to begin with, to let them know: try not to be so emotional.

Depending upon the case, you get into the details of what their issues are, and you would discuss their issues. That's the main thing, and you absolutely have to ask them what is their goal, and then you see if it is to be vindictive or, "No, it's more important for me to have custody." You see what their main concerns are, and then you go from there.

Tip from Judy Ritts, Texas Attorney at Law

The first one, which doesn't always happen first, but the first tip is hire the best lawyer you can afford. You may or may not need all of that lawyer's expertise but you can't make up for it later. If you do need it you know that that expertise is there. Hire the best lawyer you can afford.

"Hire the best lawyer you can afford. You may or may not need all of that lawyer's expertise but you

can't make up for it later."

Second one, which actually often occurs before the first one happens, is talk to a lawyer before you start negotiating with your spouse. To give an example, I had a client one time who said, "Oh we've agreed on everything. He's going to pay me $600 a month in child support," and I said, "Well, that's good. How much does he make?" And I calculated that he should be paying her $900 a month in child support. So immediately they had a big fight. You need to talk to a lawyer, find out what the law is and find out what your rights are. Find out what's reasonable to expect before you start making deals. Now once you know what the lay of the land is then you're welcome to go negotiate and see what you can settle without the help of an attorney. I'm fine with that. You've got to know what your rights are first, because I've had a lot of people call me and they've already given away some of what they don't need to give away. When they find that out then they're mad either at themselves or their spouse. It just creates more conflict later. Talk to a lawyer before you start negotiating.

The third tip I thought about is more difficult to describe. It's to find ways of preparing yourself physically, emotionally, mentally to co-parent your kids without the agreement and necessary support from your soon to be ex-spouse. That means you've got to find a way to not make disparaging remarks about the other parent. You can't use your kids as messengers either for, "I'll pick you up Tuesday at 4:00 for your dentist appointment." You really can't use your kids to do that stuff. You need to remember that accommodation really helps kids. If you have to change the possession schedule to accommodate his out-of-town business trip, don't punish him for that. You should invite each other to events, to parties in case they don't know about the Christmas pageant at school. You need to keep each other informed about medical and educational kinds of issues. If your child's going to start Catechism classes, make sure the other parent knows that so that they too can accommodate that activity. You need to not use your kids as a weapon. Accommodate the other party's needs to be with their kids and to live their life. Nothing works perfectly on a schedule.

The last one in terms of preparing yourself to co-parent is you cannot blame your ex for your lack of funds. If you need to get a job, get a job. It's not his fault that you don't make as much money as he does. It's not her fault that you have to pay child support. Yeah, you made a baby so you got to pay child support.

Don't blame each other and particularly don't blame your ex-spouse in front of your kids. Please don't do that. It's very harmful to kids.

Tip from Bernard Rinella, Attorney at Law (Firm of Rinella and Rinella)

I would say tell your lawyer everything, don't withhold any information or possible evidence because it's unfavorable or embarrassing to you. You've got to let your attorney have this information rather than the opposing counsel because you don't want to be caught by surprise. In some instances, it's better for your lawyer to bring this evidence up prior to the opposition, so it's in front of the court, and you've taken away the element of surprise there too. That's one thing I definitely tell clients, tell the lawyer everything that you know, don't conceal anything.

"Don't withhold any information or possible evidence because it's unfavorable or perhaps embarrassing to you."

I can tell them a lot of things. One is, don't be concerned that your lawyer is friendly with the opposing counsel. Too many of my clients would say, "Well you know that guy too well", etc., etc. The fact is that, if a lawyer is friendly with the opposition, it's beneficial to both parties. Your lawyer obviously has a duty to represent you and do the best he can, but the fact that he might know the other lawyer and be friendly with him is an advantage to both parties in that it removes a lot of barriers, and if the lawyers are civil toward each other, the case can be resolved a lot quicker without the animosity that sometimes is involved between counsel. So don't be concerned about that because it usually works in your favor.

There are a couple other things that I noticed when I was thinking about this. I think I would say to this person, "Have your lawyer take you to court prior to your required appearance," so that you get an idea of what the court is like, know what the courtroom is like and also if possible, the judge that might be hearing your case. That way you'd be a lot less intimidated when you appear for the first time before the judge.

Another thing I'd say is, don't take advice from anyone other than your lawyer or whoever he might refer you to. Don’t seek advice from people who have been divorced, I get this all the time. Don’t read about a divorce in the papers. Or listen to friends who have been divorced. Their intentions may be good but they are in no position to give you advice. No one cares, no one knows your case better than your lawyer, obviously, or knows the facts and laws involved and can give you the best advice. So don't listen to any other people, because they tend to give you false impressions of what's going on.

Here's an easy one, but impossible. Don't waste your time, or money, trying to contest and pursue matters that are emotional in nature rather than substance of nature. It's not easy to attempt to take emotion out of the process, but if you're able to do that, you'll be far happier and in the long run and your case will be resolved quicker.

Another one might be, and this is common, understanding the frustration that may arise. Let me start with this: This is pre-trials, and the lawyers typically go back in the chamber itself. Understand it frustrates, as frustrating as it may be, that you will not likely be able to talk to the judge at a pre-trial, because most judges don't want to talk to litigants in a pre-trial and they want to talk only to counsel. The reason is, litigants are so emotionally involved with their own cases that they don't address the legal issues that the judge is looking to hear and they don't assist the judge in resolving the case. So this frustration may appear to the litigant, but it's really working in the litigant's best interest that the judge only hears from the attorneys.

CHAPTER THREE

WHAT IF SOMEONE IS FIGHTING FOR CHILD CUSTODY?

Tip from Irene Intelligator, Attorney at Law

I've been handling divorces for 30 years. My first tip, always has been and remains, keep in mind that when you compromise, you always win, especially if you have children. Even if you give up a little bit more than you initially seemed to be willing to, you will, ultimately, still win because when you go to court, only lawyers win every way. You never know what the judge will do. Ultimately, it's always a crap shoot, and when you're willing to compromise, you may not get exactly what you want, but you have a certain measure of control in the outcome. There are times that it's just not possible because the other side is a complete jerk, but when it is at all possible, then you always try to compromise.

"When you compromise, you will always win,

especially if you have children."

I make a lot more money going to court, and I can be very aggressive if I need to be. For me, this is advice from my heart. I truly mean it because I make a lot more money when I go to court than if people settle, and we just do it nice. Think about it. If you go to court, you can sit there all day. The hearing starts at 8:30, but it never starts at 8:30. You're lucky if it starts at like 10:00.

It's like a tab. It's like the time is ticking, and you're not getting anywhere. You're just sitting there paying for nothing.

As for child custody where there is say, one child between the couple, I would tell them that there are circumstances where 50-50 is okay, and it works. There are circumstances where it just does not work, so you really have to know your child. Ultimately, the goal is for a person, for a little person, or a teenager, whoever the child is, if they'll spend frequent and continuous time with both parents. That's the goal. That's a stated goal for the state of California, and the court will try to pursue it as much as the court can. Ultimately, know your child and make sure you are not trying to just screw the other party by spending more time with the kid when you never really had before. Ultimately, you're hurting the child. Really, know your child and see, truly, what is in the child's best interest, and then try to fashion a plan that'll work for the child best interest. Don’t do it to hurt the other parent.

Tip from Seth D. Kramer, Esq CFLS (Certified Family Law Specialist)

The first thing that I would tell someone to do is to obtain copies of their tax return and as many records of assets such as bank accounts, savings accounts, brokerage accounts, that exist and that they would have access to. For example, some spouses may say, "Well, my spouse has all these records in a file cabinet in the bedroom." I would say either make a copy of all those so that you have those, so at least we would know what exists. The other thing is I would tell the person that they need to approach this from a cost benefit analysis. Even though custody of the children and issues dealing with children may be priceless, you still have to put a real world figure on it. Figure on litigating it and determining what you want to do with it, depending on the realities of the entire situation. If your concern about your child is such that, "This is not the person I married," either this person went through some kind of transformation and is a monster, then clearly you have to make appropriate decisions based on that.

One of the things you need to be concerned with is the entire economics of the entire estate and situation, meaning that you don't necessarily want to spend all your money and time just to do one part of what you're concerned with. Assuming how long the marriage has been, you don't necessarily want to destroy or spend all of the assets just scorching the earth. The third thing I would tell the person, which is similar to the second thing, would be to address this maturely. Don't have anger issues cloud what your determinations are.

"Obtain copies of tax returns and as many records of assets such as bank accounts, savings accounts, brokerage

accounts, that exist."

You need to look at this thing coldly and then impassionately so that you can make proper and appropriate decisions. That's what I will advise, I will give them dispassionate advice, and I would like them to respond to it appropriately, taking into considerations of all of those things that I mentioned.

If they have a couple of children, I would ask them if they worked out some arrangement with the other spouse as to what's going to happen with the children in connection with them splitting up. If they haven't then I would explore to see if they can discuss some arrangement so that at least the children are taken care of.

In California, the law is that absence is something really not in the children's best interests, the court will basically accept any kind of resolution regarding child custody that the parties have worked out. They can't have something like boiling the kid in oil and expect the Court to sign off on that, but something where it appears to be reasonable then the Court won't necessarily substitute their judgment for the parents', and if this works for the parents based on their situation, based on what's best for the children, and both the parents are in agreement with it, the Courts generally almost rubber stamp that. I hasten to use the word rubber stamp, because the Court is involved in making certain that the arrangements are in the children's best interest, but absence of the extraordinary, the Courts would defer to the parents' determination of best interest.

Tip from Michael Griffin, Attorney at Law

The first and most important thing is take the high road. They're always angry. They're always upset. They've lost a great deal, usually emotionally. The first thing you tell them is, "No fooling around. No stalking people. No social media stuff. Remember, everything you do from now on will wind up in a district in front of a judge or jury, so be on your best behavior. I know you're mad, but take the high road."

Number two would be, along with taking the high road, in Texas, we have community property, and you're probably entitled to half of whatever you got, but at this point in time, you're under the jurisdiction of a district court.

"Everything you do from now on will wind up in a district in front of a judge or jury, so be on your best behavior."

Let's not be stalling the boat. Let's not be taking dad's hunting rifles and hiding them, or any of that stuff. It's half yours. It's half hers. Let the judge decide. No games with titles, real estate, or anything like that.

As far as child custody, first and foremost, they need to understand that in Texas there's no longer a presumption that the mother is the best custodial caretaker, so that's gone. It can be dad, but you're going to have to prove it, Dad. That means when you get temporary visitation and possession and access, you be there on time with no bullshit, and you do what the judge is telling you to do. Then, when we go and try and get you custody based on the other stuff, I don't have to deal with the fact that you were in a bar with your friends instead of being with the kid at 6:30 on Thursday night.

Tip from Belinda C. Brown, Attorney at Law

The top two tips are to watch what they're doing on social media and to do everything possible to keep it amicable, not to intentionally push the other spouse's buttons because that won't help anyway. Sometimes, people put things on social media that aren't even true to try and impress other people, but that can come up and be used in court.

"Watch what you're doing on social media and do everything

possible to keep it amicable."

They usually follow my advice, but I've seen people who, before they hired me, posted pictures of them having a drinking party or just pictures of them drinking and carrying on, and the children are in the picture. That's evidence that you can't put back in the bottle. That genie's out at that point. They're going to have to deal with the fact that they can't go and claim to the judge that they are not partying in front of the child. That was one of the other spouse's complaints.

Let's say the couple has a couple kids, have been married ten years, here are some tips for that?

First, it depends on some factors. If the children are old enough for their choice to be relevant, then I want their honesty, at that point, not what they would wish, but what they actually expect the children's choice would be. Sometimes, you can head off a lot of arguing if you really know that even though you like to have your kids live with you, that they really want to live with, say, the father of the client. If the kids really wanted their daughters, and they really want to live with mom, it's probably not going to be a battle you're going to win if the children want to be with her and if they're over 12.

CHAPTER FOUR

WHAT IF SOMEONE IS FIGHTING FOR CHILD SUPPORT?

Tip from Scott D. Reiner, Attorney at Law

First ask contested or uncontested. Ask for the property. What is the property like? Is it going to be how they contest it or can we expect to reach an agreement? Just know there'll be injunctions issued, they'll have to pay regardless of the status of the marriage and residence.

Child support's basically formulaic. It's all based on the earnings. It also depends on which parent is the primary. Parties can also agree to set a certain amount, but for a family agreement it will be set basically according to the formula in the law.

Tip from Paul J. Duron, Attorney at Law

The first thing I always ask and I would probably advise is if they've spoken to their spouse about contemplating filing a divorce. Not only talking about the idea of divorce, but more specifically the issue that would need to be addressed if they do divorce, main ones being child custody, how visitation would go, child support, the possibility of spousal support, division of property, things like that, having a much more thorough conversation than, "I want the marriage to end."

Here in California, I don't know how other states do it, but here we do have a California Statutory Guideline Amount, which is specifically a calculation. I explain to them that we do have that calculation, that child support is based on two major factors, which is the income of the parties and then the timeshare that each of them has with the children. Depending which side you're looking at, then timeshare is very important for especially the non-custodial parent, if they're intending not to pay such a high child support amount.

Tip from the Law Offices of Fran Brochstein

Child Support - For someone going through a divorce in Texas and wanting to know about child support, they need to first look at their tax returns. In Texas, we take into account all sources of income also known as "net resources" (it's defined in the Texas Family Code). For example, I've actually had people that don't "work". I said, "Okay, how do you live and pay your bills?" For example, one man owned several blocks of downtown Houston. He lived off of his investments. Well, his child support will be based on his income based on his tax returns. He was a multi-millionaire. He was not happy about having to pay child support because he did not actually "work".

What most people don't realize is that other people have tried every trick in the book. At the courthouse is a syndrome referred to as "RAIDS" or "Recently Acquired Income Deficiency Syndrome". The best example I have of that is, if I had an engineer quit his job, making over $200,000 a year. He decided to become a bagger at a grocery store making minimum wage. We went down, and the judge said, "I think it is lovely that you are a bagger at a grocery store. You are purposely underemployed and therefore you are going to pay child support at your last job at $200,000 a year." Needless to say, the guy was upset.

I had an oil executive that got laid off in the oil business. I said, "Okay, so are you going to go get another job?" He said, "Yeah." I said, "Okay, it will be based on your new job." He was upset and wanted it based on his unemployment. Judges know that most oil executives get new jobs and they are willing to wait a few months until the person gets a new full-time job with benefits.

Child Custody & Spousal Support - Since Texas is a gender neutral state, I've had at least 3 women in the last year that had "house husbands" that they supported 100% because the men were home raising the children while the wife worked. In all 3 cases, the men qualified for spousal support. I thought men paying spousal support were angry until I observed these women's reactions.

Many people are under the mistaken belief that Texas does not have alimony. The legislature of Texas opened that door several years ago and the door is getting opened wider every time the Texas legislature meets. Texas is not as generous as California, but Texas has now opened the door.

Many women mistakenly believe that they get automatic custody in Texas of the minor children. Again, the Texas legislature modified the Texas Family Code many years ago to be gender neutral. Having given birth does not automatically insure that a woman will win primary custody. Perhaps some courts lean more toward giving a mother custody of a small baby but the law is technically gender neutral.

Any man that says a male cannot get custody in Texas is wrong! Approx. 20 years ago I started getting men custody of their children. I would screen the men that came to be carefully but I frequently was able to get the male primary custody of the minor children. I agree that a man has a harder burden than a female, but I've seen it done often in the Harris County courthouses. And, in mediation the parties often switch custody when a child reaches puberty. After practicing law over 25 years, many men make good "mommies"!

Another term I often hear is that people want "full custody" of a child. I have no idea that that means since it is not a legal term used in Texas. It is presumed in the Texas Family Code that the parents will co-parent and that they will both have Joint Custody of the minor children. Joint custody does not mean that there will be no child support. Joint custody does not mean that the parents will equally share the children. I urge people to talk to an experienced family law attorney when the first begin to think about separating or divorcing.

Why Mediation Works - I'm always shocked at a mediation when an attorney has not prepared the client for the reality of divorce and child custody cases. Many people have unrealistic expectations of what actually happens in mediation and at trial in front of a judge. I believe that attorneys do a disservice to their clients but not "reality testing" throughout their legal representation with their clients. Sometimes clients need to hear things that they don't want to hear. Clients need to understand the reality of divorce and child custody laws in the State of Texas. There are no winners in the family courts – the children are the biggest losers. If there are any winners it's the lawyers because they make a lot of money off letting people "fight" at the courthouse. So while the clients are draining their bank accounts the attorneys are filling theirs!

I have been told repeatedly by Texas judges that they never give anyone 100% because they do not want one party to feel like they "won". Judges prefer to give each party "something" and have both leave unhappy. Since judges in Texas are elected, judges are very sensitive to trying to be fair and impartial to all parties.

Also, even though it's alleged often I know of no family judge in Harris County has that been "bought off". When I dig a little deeper with the unhappy person, I find that they did not get everything they wanted and expected so they think that the opposing attorney "paid off" the judge.

In mediation I frequently find out more about the case then their own attorney because I ask a lot of questions. That's how I settle cases at mediation, because I actually listen to the people discuss their feelings and their fears. Fear, anger, revenge, and other emotions can often paralyze a person. A person that is in panic mode cannot make rational and reasonable decisions. A person's feelings must be addressed in order to help them make decisions that they will not regret later and move forward. Some attorneys try to avoid discussing emotions and feelings. In order to be an effective mediator, I must address what is motivating the people and their feelings.

When I litigated, I often had judges ask me why I never had contested hearings and trials in their courtroom. I would tell them that I know how they are going to rule in a case and I can therefore usually settle a case without going to mediation or trial. A good attorney knows the judge and the judge's approach to applying the law. Even though the State of Texas only has one Family Code, the code is interpreted by the Judge. Every judge is different and each judge has their own interpretation of the law.

Plus:

Advice to people going through a divorce or modification

I tell people do not talk to everyone about what you're going through, because after a while you get really boring and people will begin to avoid you. Then I tell people that they should immediately go into therapy to get them through this difficult period I also can assure them that if they work really, really hard on themselves then two years from now they'll be in a much better place and much happier.

What Judges say about talking "bad" about the other parent

One judge recently told me that 2's don't marry 10's. The best example I'd like to give is when a woman says, "You know, I've got 4 kids, my husband's a drug addict, he doesn't work, he sleeps all the time and plays video games." I said to them, "I'm sorry. You chose to stay with him all these years, and have more than one child with him. The bottom line, when you go in front of the judge to complain about him, how does that reflect well on your selection process?" It shows very poor judgement and common sense on your part. People are appalled when I say that, but more than one judge told me that they picked each other and they have to live with the decisions that they have made.

For example, several years ago one mother and father got on the stand and said how bad the other parent was. The judge stopped the process and said, "Here's the bottom line. I believe both of you. I'm calling CPS and your children are immediately going into CPS (TX Children's Protective Services) custody." I was at the courthouse that morning and the word spread like wildfire about what the judge had done in the case. That afternoon, I got a phone call from the mommy, and she and daddy were now the best of friends because their kids were in CPS custody. I said to her, "I already heard about your case and I'm not interested unless you show up in my office with $15,000 and understand that it will probably take 6 months or more to get your children back home." She was like, "We don't have that kind of money." I said, "You guys decided to sling the mud and say how bad the other parent was, and the judge determined that you were both telling the truth so she is obligated to protect your children." These parents had to go through a lot of time, money and almost a year of being supervised by CPS and completing the CPS parenting plan (supervised visits with their children, drug tests, therapy, parenting classes, home inspections, etc.) to get their children back home.

Reality of Family Law in Texas Courts

People don't understand that good attorneys resolve most of their cases, if they cannot resolve their case then the attorneys go to a mediator for help in trying to settle the case. If the mediator cannot settle the case, then the Judge hears the case. So if you think about it, Judges see the worst of the worst of people in their county. Judges dockets are huge and judges don't have the time to hear every case. In reality, in the Houston area, approximately 90% of all cases are resolved without a judge ever hearing the matter. Most attorneys will never admit it but almost every family law case settles – very few attorneys have trials these days.

Surprise Divorces

I have often seen one spouse has been unhappy for a long time and eventually something happens (usually it's minor) that makes them file for divorce. When the other spouse is served with divorce papers they are shocked because they had no idea that their marriage was in trouble. Some people have not fought in years and often they have not even spoken to each other for a long time. At least when people are fighting they are still attempting to communicate. The party that is unhappy wants a quick divorce so they can move on with their life. The other party is in shock and wants to "save" the marriage. I find that good attorneys encourage the unhappy party to be patient and gradually help the other party realize that the divorce is inevitable. I often encourage both parties to go to counseling – not to stay married but to learn how to be divorced in a healthy way.

How People should act when their relationship is ending

When spouses have children, I always encourage people to take the high road and never talk bad about their spouse to the children. I remind people that the children are 50% of each of them and when they insult the other parent then they are also insulting the child. I encourage them to never discuss "adult business" with the child – even if the "child" is an adult. It is the child's job to be their child and it is the parent's job to act like adults and do what is in their child's best interests. If both parents are unhappy and the child is doing well then the parents are obviously doing something right.

My parents divorced when I was in my early 30's and a divorce attorney. I tell people that I don't care if you are 3, 13, 23 or 33, when your parents divorce it is horrible. The children of the marriage (and perhaps even grand-children) also need time to adjust to this new dynamic. I assure people that it takes a while but if everyone stays flexible and open-minded then everyone can adjust to the new arrangement.

I say you should always take the high road in dealing with the other person. Why? So that you can look at yourself in the mirror 2 years from now, and if something bad happens to the other person you know you did the right thing.

Social Media Warning

With the internet, new areas of conflict are occurring – such as social media harassment and stalking. People post the most unbelievably damaging things on social media. I've seen death threats, admissions of illegal activities, selfies of drunk people, etc. Many attorneys are now including in their legal services agreement that a person will not post anything on any social media site while the attorney represents the person. My advice, stay off of social media – especially if you have had an alcoholic beverage or lack of sleep.

I recently did a mediation, and the wife's alcohol consumption was an issue. The husband walks in with social media posts that had been posted within the last 24 hours. The night before our mediation the wife and her mother posted photos of them drinking in bar. I went to her mother and said, "You knew alcohol was a huge factor in this divorce, and the two of you were in a bar last night?" Her Mom replied "Well, we only had two or three beers." I looked at her and pulled up her Facebook page, all the photos were of the mother in bars drinking. (There were no photos of the children or anything other than bar photos.) I said, "Here's the bottom line. Every time you get drunk, you go on Facebook. Let me give you a hint. Next time before you walk into the bar, turn off your phone."

I recently had an unusual experience at a mediation, the husband showed me his cell phone with vile text messages from the wife. I got permission from the husband to show the wife. (I have them in separate rooms because of domestic violence allegations.) I show them to her, and she's like, "I never sent any of those." I said, "Well, let me see your phone." It's a different phone number. A lot of people buy burner phones, so I got my cell phone out, and I dialed the number that apparently the messages were coming from, and the guy's briefcase rang. Husband's attorney was quiet and this case settled quickly.

My personal story

I'm on marriage #3 so hopefully I've learned a few things. I've also been a Texas attorney approx. 25 years and I've been doing family law for 20 years. My kid is over 30, and I still talk to my ex-husband all the time. We planned a wedding together – my ex, his wife and me. After I divorced, my child was very little and we had a lot of problems. I thought getting a divorce would solve my problems, but it did not. It merely changed my problems. So we went to therapy for 2 years. It was the best money we could have spent. We had to learn how to co-parent. The counselor we saw urged us to learn to co-parent. As I tell people, if you work hard then things will get better.

At my daughter's high school graduation party my daughter stood up and thanked her dad and I for never putting her in the middle. She said that she was the only child of divorced parents that was only having one graduation party – most of her friends had to have 2 parties because their parents could not be in the same room with each other. How sad – especially for the child.

In Summary

Remember, once you have children you are never truly divorced. You will co-parent your children and your future grand-children for the rest of your lives. At one time, you obviously loved the other parent and now things have changed between you, but that does not mean that either of you can quit being a parent or caring about your child. I encourage people to put their kid's first and everything else second.

Tip from Maria Testa, Attorney at Law

I always address the children first because normally that really is what everybody wants to discuss first. Then of course secondary to that are the assets.

The first thing you really tell somebody is, separate your money now because the first part of divorce, typically, is the worst part, when everything starts to get moving, when somebody files something or when somebody says, "Okay, I'm going to hire an attorney tomorrow and I'm going to file something." Everybody is scared of the unknown and so the first thing that they do is either empty bank accounts out or they just stop paying joint bills that they're paying through their own bank account.

"Separate your money now because the first part of divorce, typically, is the worst part."

Protecting what you have in the bank is important because you don't get that back until the end in equitable distribution. First the children, and then second I usually say make sure that you separate your assets and your income.

If you have direct deposit into a joint account, make sure you change it before your next paycheck. You really aren't supposed to touch things like savings accounts or things like that. It depends, if it's a single parent or a non-working spouse I will tell them, "Okay. Take half out. Put it in your own account because that's what you're going to likely be entitled to in the end." You're not doing anything wrong, but you have to protect yourself f really before the other side does something. Those are the first two things that I would say I discuss with someone.

Before you separate, if you can, if you have access to it, get the tax return, because oftentimes people run their own business. A lot of people are self-employed, a lot of people are contractors and they get paid under the table. Get the tax returns before you don't have access to them or they claim their lost or you have to send subpoenas and spend more money to get them.

The way that child support works, though, it doesn't matter how long you've been married, you get it until the child is eighteen or graduates high school in

Pennsylvania, which can happen sooner. In terms of spousal support, it's really, really important to make people understand two things: if you were a stay-at-home parent and your children are no longer minors, you better start looking for a job because the court is starting to move away from, "Okay, this is a stay-at-home parent. They're going to get lifetime alimony and that's it." They don't really think that way anymore. It's more, everybody has an obligation now to really support their child and so you better start brushing up on your skills and looking for a job.

CHAPTER FIVE

WHAT IF SOMEONE IS FIGHTING FOR SPOUSAL MAINTENANCE?

Tip from Annette Fernholz, Attorney at Law

That would depend on which party was coming to talk to me. By that, I mean, which party has access to cash or credit, or some funds. If the person coming to me does not have access, isn't the bread-winner, doesn't have a paycheck, one of the first things I tell them to do is to try and get their hands on some money, because the court system takes 30, 60, 90 days, before it would likely award them any funds. In that particular case, if they're a party who doesn't have access or doesn't earn income, then that's my number one tip or concern for that person. I also generally tell them to try to keep things as pleasant as can be possible with the other party when the children are present, or in the presence of the children, because their acrimony shouldn't be taking place in front of the children.

If I represent the monied party, I generally tell them not to cut the other person off from health insurance, life insurance, or any other benefits that are currently in place for that person.

Let's say they cut their spouse's health insurance, and that person went and needed an appendectomy. Now you have an uncovered person with an eight-thousand, twelve-thousand-dollar medical bill, for the entire marital estate to pay. You really have to be careful about doing any harsh, immediate, knee-jerk reactions. That's one of the things I try to caution them against.

"Acrimony shouldn't be taking place in front of the children."

As far as a tip for someone who knows that they're going to have to pay maintenance or be paid, I say this. That makes a big difference who you're representing. Generally, if you're representing someone who hasn't worked for a number of years, it depends upon how long the marriage is. If they haven't worked for a number of years, I don't necessarily run out and tell them to take just any job, if they're uneducated. I may tell people to go to school to brush up on their skills, those kinds of things. In Illinois, they have a new maintenance statute, which tells people the duration of maintenance. It's formulaic now, what they would receive, depending upon what the other party earns, and what they earn. Definitely don't tell anybody to quit their job. That would not be my advice to anybody.

Tip from Evie Jeang, Attorney at Law

When a client comes into my house or office for a consultation and tells me they want to get divorced, I always ask them if they can sit down with the other person and really nail down the issues they would raise in arguments. Family law attorneys get paid by billable hour, not by a flat fee. It's the most cost-effective way for both parties to really figure out what issues they need an attorney to help with. Depending on the outcome of that meeting, they shouldn't spend money on an attorney since getting a divorce is already emotionally stressful and adding financial stress can make the divorce process even more difficult.

I always say, "Before you come back and we start this paperwork, sit down with your wife or husband, have a nice glass of wine and say, 'Hey, this marriage is not working. What do you think that we should do from here? What can we agree on? What can't we agree on?'" So when they actually go back to the attorney's office, they have a more organized worksheet about what they need their attorney to help with, saving them both time and money. That's number one.

The second piece of advice I always give is to keep a record of everything. That means keeping a calendar—

track how often you see the kids, where you take them, to what daycare, who takes them to the daycare, doctor's appointments, etc. Highlight the time you spend with the kids because when you're getting divorced, if you have children, custody is one of the biggest issues. You want to show the court how often you spend time with the kids. Having a very basic calendar, or even printing off a Microsoft Outlook calendar will show your time with the kids. It's very easy to read and the judge will like that.

"Keep a record of everything."

The third thing I would say that can be very helpful in the case that you have to go to litigation, which can be very expensive, is to consider first going to mediation. You can get a retired judge or a very experienced family law attorney who is a specialist to sit down with both parties and try to work out the dispute issues. Instead of each party paying the attorney and paying separate billable hours, you can get someone who has both legal experience and familiarity with helping two people resolve their issues. This way, you're only paying for one person, instead of having each person pay for their own attorney. When you have one attorney trying to mediate between two parties, I think it makes the process less hostile, and it's a much more cooperative and compromising setting. These are the top three things that come to mind when discussing divorce. It really makes the dynamic less hostile, and it also saves money. My main goal for clients is to try to save them money because oftentimes, people can become hostile in the divorce process and fight over unnecessary things.

Question: What is your number one tip for someone coming in worried about spousal maintenance, from both the point of view of the husband and the wife?

As far as spousal maintenance, I can't speak for the husband, but women nowadays are making good money. I have a client where the woman is actually paying the spousal support to the husband. Whomever the higher earner is, should really consider whether divorce is the best option. You can't just say, "I'm mad at you. Our marriage is failing. I'm going to try to show you by filing a divorce." You really have to spread it out and think it through for a year or so.

For the high earners, I would be prepared to show that your lifestyle is not as great, nor as high as your spouse's, since part of spousal support is calculated based on income and lifestyle. If you're a high earner, I would be wary of how you spend your money—a key factor when getting divorced. Take Warren Buffett for example—he is an extremely wealthy person, yet he lives very humbly, so lifestyle makes a difference. From the other party who's receiving the support, I would try to establish lifestyle and show why you need the support.

If you're a stay-at-home mom or a stay-at-home dad raising the kids, it's very easy for you to get support because you haven't been in the workforce for a while. However, the support isn't going to last forever, unless it's a long term marriage, and eventually, you will need to find a job. Again, it depends on what kind of marriage we're talking about because some people have more money, which means they have a grander lifestyle, while on the other hand, most people just want to maintain a normal family. I have a client whose family has a private jet. For her, the typical spousal support wouldn't fit, so how is she going to argue? It comes down to lifestyle.

Average American people establish support based on income. Again, if I'm the supporting party, I would try to downsize my lifestyle considerably. Don't spend more than you earn. I think that a lot of people tend to do that. If I'm the one who's trying to receive support, then obviously I'm going to try and argue for lifestyle, the need to get support and why. For example I would say, "I've been raising both children all these years and I have been out of the job market for so long. I do eventually want to go back to the job market, but I will definitely need support first, at least for the first couple of years, until I can get back on my feet."

Tip from Rick Marsh, Attorney at Law

First of all, if you're an attorney, you're supposed to try to see if there's any chance that the couple can reconcile, so you establish that right off the bat. You say, "Hey, is there any chance of this working out? Is there some kind of counseling? Is there some type of therapy? AA? Whatever the problem might be, is there something that can be done to salvage this?" That's the first thing you do.

Second thing depends on the situation. If there's physical assault going on, you're going to have to get a temporary restraining order.

"Whatever the problem might be, is there something

that can be done to salvage this?"

If it's simply a matter of finances, you might want to get some kind of restraining order to stop people from doing something with the stocks, bonds, funds, bank accounts, stuff like that. Each situation is different and needs to be treated differently. Sometimes it's just about custody. You have to analyze what the problem is, and then you try to rectify it.

In Texas, we have a thing called alimony, but it's rarely applied. You have to be married more than ten years. Even though there's provision for it in the code, judges rarely give it. The only times that they will give that would be, basically, if a wife has been a homemaker all along, the whole time, and never really got a chance to get into the job world. Sometimes, with a long marriage, they'll give some alimony for that. We don't really use alimony much in Texas. It's mainly child support.

Tip from Paul F. Moore II, Attorney at Law

There are two or three things that come to mind. Is there a threat of violence? Are you in personal jeopardy if you say, "I'm leaving." Number two, any threat of concealing or harming the child? And number three, do you suspect that your spouse will take steps to conceal assets?

Let's say you've been married ten years and you ask me about spousal maintenance. I'm in California, and in California ten years is a magic number. And it's not definitive, but we have a rule that a marriage of ten years or longer is considered a long-term marriage. Shorter than ten years is considered a short-term marriage. And that has maintenance, or we call it spousal support but maintenance is the same, and it implicates that. If somebody came to me and they were right on the cusp of ten years, I would want to know if they are likely to be the payor spouse or likely to be the payee spouse. And if they are the payor, they might want to, if they have decided that they are going to file for a divorce, or if it's inevitable, try to get in under the ten-year line.

And as I say, it's not definitive that a court could determine that a marriage of less than ten years is nevertheless long-term, and a court could say that a marriage slightly longer than ten years is also a short-term marriage. But courts in California generally follow that. The difference is this: If your marriage is determined to be a long-term marriage; a court cannot terminate spousal support or maintenance without being able to clearly articulate how the supported spouse will be able to support themselves.

So if somebody has a trust fund then it's not a big deal necessarily. Or somebody is coming into money with them then the court might say, "Well you're going to have maintenance for two or three years until your trust activates," or something like that. But if it's more than ten years and it's not clear, then it would be an abuse of discretion for the court to terminate spousal support within a finite term. If it's more than ten years and they said, "You're going to pay support or receive support for four years and that will give you time to get a job and get on your feet, and good luck," that would be reversible in California without clear facts that would indicate the receiving spouse would be able to support themselves.

So that's why that ten-year line is crucial. Here's another California legislative maxim: For short-term marriages it's presumed that a supported spouse will be able to support themselves within a reasonable period of time. A reasonable period of time is considered half the length of the marriage. So, let's say you've been married eight years. You can kind of count on spousal support maybe for four. There's a wide swath of judicial discretion in support and lots of individual facts might color it.

Made in the USA
Monee, IL
04 November 2026

67385540R10066